COUNTRY INSIGHTS
JAPAN

Nick Bornoff

WAYLAND

COUNTRY INSIGHTS

BRAZIL • CHINA • FRANCE • JAMAICA • JAPAN • KENYA • MEXICO • PAKISTAN

GUIDE TO THIS BOOK

As well as telling you about the whole of Japan, this book looks closely at the city of Okazaki and the village of Narai.

 This city symbol will appear at the top of the page and information boxes each time Okazaki is looked at.

This rural symbol will appear each time Narai is looked at.

Cover photograph: Two boys ready to play baseball, Japan's national sport.

Title page: Catching some early summer sun on Shikoku Island.

Contents page: Mount Fuji, on the main island of Honshu, is Japan's highest mountain. It is also a sleeping volcano, which last erupted in 1707. Mount Fuji is seen as sacred by many Japanese.

Book and series editor: Polly Goodman
Book designers: Mark Whitchurch/Malcolm Walker
Series designer: Tim Mayer
Production controller: Caroline Davis
Consultant: Dr Tony Binns, Geography lecturer and tutor of student teachers at the University of Sussex.

First published in 1996 by
Wayland Publishers Ltd
61 Western Road, Hove
East Sussex, BN3 1JD, England

British Library Cataloguing in Publication Data
Bornoff, Nicholas
    Japan. – (Country Insights)
    1. Japan – Juvenile literature
    I. Title
    952'. 049

ISBN 0 7502 2011 2

Typeset by Mark Whitchurch, England
Printed and bound in Italy by LEGO S.p.A., Vicenza.

Contents

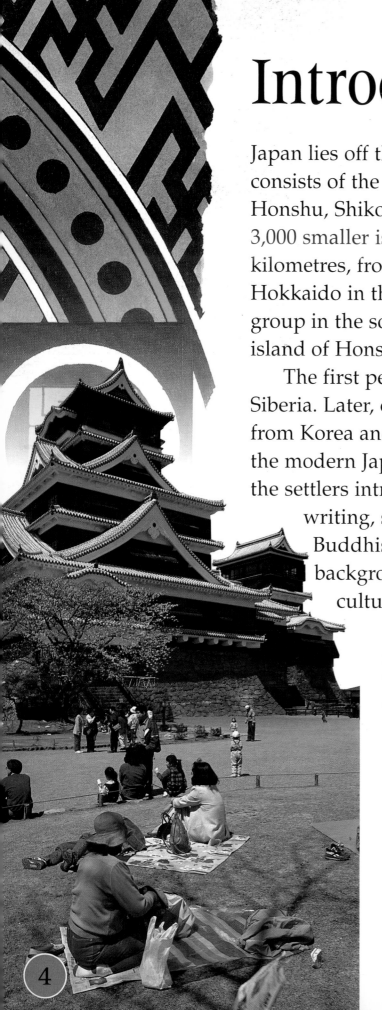

Introducing Japan

Japan lies off the east coast of mainland Asia, and consists of the four main islands of Hokkaido, Honshu, Shikoku and Kyushu. There are also over 3,000 smaller islands, spread over a distance of 2,500 kilometres, from the isolated islands north of Hokkaido in the north-east, to the sunny Ryukyu group in the south. The capital, Tokyo, is on the main island of Honshu.

The first people of Japan probably came from Siberia. Later, over many centuries, settlers arrived from Korea and China. These were the ancestors of the modern Japanese. Beginning with rice farming, the settlers introduced Chinese civilization, including writing, science, art, architecture and the Buddhist religion. From this mixed background, the Japanese developed a culture of their own.

The Japanese balance ancient and modern ways of life together. They believe in Shinto, a religion that dates back to prehistoric times. When the Buddhist religion arrived, 1,300 years ago, the two religions began to be practised side by side. Today, many colourful festivals all over the country celebrate the religion of Shinto.

Kumamoto Castle is one of many old samurai fortresses that are dotted about Japan.

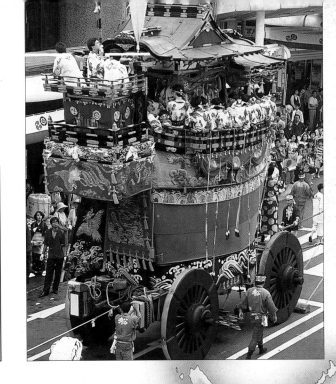

Kyoto's three-day Gion Matsuri festival ▶
attracts hundreds of thousands of people.
One of the highlights of the festival is a
parade of floats through the city streets.

JAPAN	
Total land area:	377,688 km²
Population:	125.9 million
Capital:	Tokyo
Highest mountain:	Mt Fuji, 3,776 m
Currency:	Yen

Source: *Facts and Figures Japan* (Foreign Press Centre, 1995)

By 1900, Japan had become the most advanced
nation in Asia. After the Second World War
(1939–1945), which devastated the country, Japan
had to rebuild its cities and industries. From the
1950s, however, Japan began to grow into
one of the wealthiest and
most technologically advanced countries in
the world. Today, Japan is the world
leader in the production of cars,
machinery and electronics,
and its wealth is second
only to the USA.

**This book will take ▶
you to the city of
Okazaki and the
village of Narai,
as well as the rest
of Japan. You can
find these places
on the map.**

HOKKAIDO

SEA OF JAPAN

HONSHU

JAPANESE ALPS

Narai
Kiso Mt Fuji
Kyoto
Nagoya △
Tokyo
Kobe
Okazaki
Yokohama

PACIFIC OCEAN

SHIKOKU

0   100   200   300   400   500 km

0   100   200   300 miles

EAST
CHINA
SEA

KYUSHU

N

RYUKYU ISLANDS

OKINAWA

Japan's place in the world

JAPAN

The city of Okazaki

Okazaki is a thriving city of 320,000 residents, which lies near the south-east coast of the main island of Honshu. It is about 80 kilometres from the busy city of Nagoya, the regional capital.

People have lived in Okazaki since prehistoric times. The city is famous for being the birthplace of Tokugawa Ieyasu (1542–1610), who was the greatest of all the shoguns, or samurai rulers. Shoguns, who were originally warriors, were military leaders who ruled Japan from 1603–1868. Ieyasu was an important shogun because he united Japan after 500 years of civil war. He then began building roads between the country's major cities. Okazaki became an important city along the main road between what is now Tokyo in the east and Kyoto in the west. This road was called the Tokaido. Ieyasu built the basis of the main road system still in use in Japan.

Okazaki during rush hour. This busy main street is part of the national expressway to Nagoya.

Okazaki's population has tripled since 1945 due to Japan's industrialization. The city was badly damaged during the war and then rebuilt, so it is now a modern city with only a few old temples still standing. Yet despite its concrete buildings and booming industries, Okazaki remains a very traditional city. There are still a large number of traditional crafts and industries in the city that are hundreds of years old. Okazaki's ability to mix old traditions with new technologies successfully make this city typically Japanese.

Fermented soybeans are made into miso paste. Miso is still prepared in Okazaki using methods that are centuries old.

The village of Narai

Narai is a sleepy village with a population of only a few hundred people, which lies in the valley of the Kiso river. This beautiful area is famous for its mountains, rivers, forests and waterfalls. Narai lies on an old mountain road, called the Nakasendo, which was once an alternative route between the cities of Edo (modern-day Tokyo) and Kyoto.

Like Okazaki, Narai used to be an important point along a major road. In 1911, however, a railway was built to connect the towns along the way, and the Nakasendo fell into disuse. As a result, Narai became increasingly remote. The village has changed very little over the past fifty years. Narai's picturesque main street, called Naraijuku, is now protected by the government from new development. Among its many attractive old wooden buildings, there are two hotels that were built over 250 years ago. In a country where everything is changing fast, that's very old indeed.

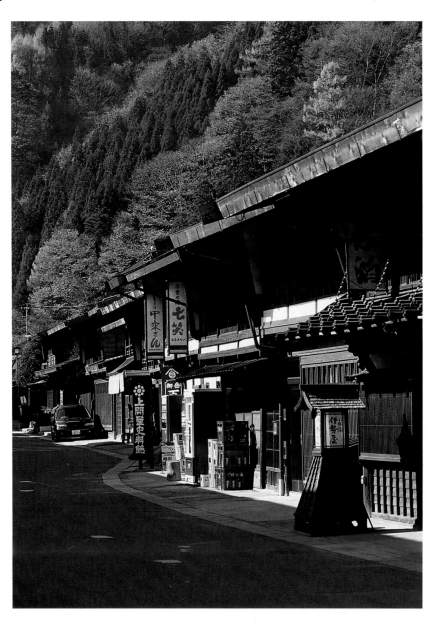

Traditional wooden houses on Narai's main street stand against the village's mountain backdrop.

8

When Japan began developing its industries after the Second World War, many people left villages in areas like the Kiso valley to seek jobs in Japan's rapidly developing cities. Today Narai, like many villages in the Kiso area, is looking increasingly towards tourism to survive.

'Our children work in Tokyo, but I would rather stay here. The city is too noisy!' – Nobuko Furukawa, 88 years old.

Over half of the residents of Narai ▶ are over sixty years old. Most of the younger generation move to the cities.

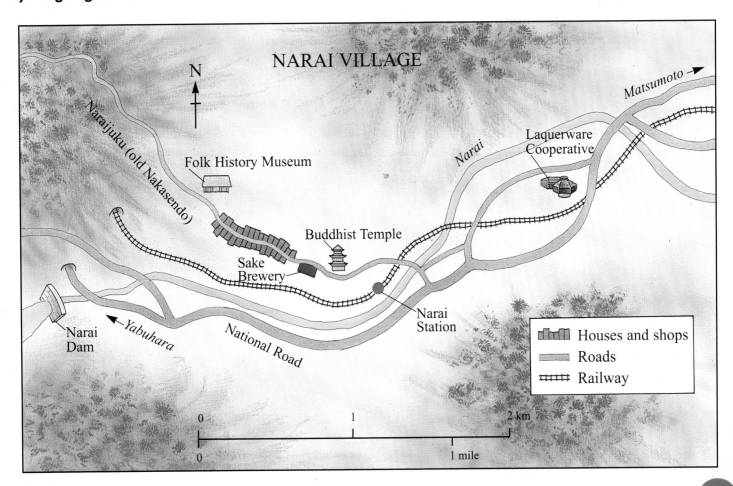

NARAI VILLAGE

N

Matsumoto ▶

Naraijuku (old Nakasendo)

Folk History Museum

Narai

Laquerware Cooperative

Buddhist Temple

Sake Brewery

Narai Station

Narai Dam

◀ Yabuhara

National Road

	Houses and shops
	Roads
	Railway

0   1   2 km

0   1 mile

Landscape and climate

The dangerously active Mt Sakurajima, in the south of Kyushu Island.

Japan has four seasons, but since it is a long, narrow chain of islands, which stretch over 2,500 kilometres, its climate differs from north to south. Conditions in the north are Siberian, with harsh, snowy winters and mild summers. Winters towards the south are gentler, but the summers are very hot and humid. All regions, except the north, have a short rainy season every year from mid-May to mid-June.

JAPAN'S CLIMATE		
	Average temperature	Average annual
	June–August Jan–March	rainfall
Sapporo, Hokkaido:	20°C –5°C	1,130 mm
Kanazawa, Honshu:	26°C 3°C	2,593 mm
Tokyo, Pacific Side:	25°C 5°C	1,405 mm
Okinawa, Riyuku Islands:	28°C 15°C	2,037 mm

Source: *Facts and Figures Japan* (Foreign Press Centre, 1995)

Lying along a fault in the earth's crust, Japan is prone to earthquakes. These can sometimes be devastating, and so far no accurate way has been found to predict them. Where there are earthquakes, there is usually volcanic activity. About one tenth of all the world's active volcanoes are in Japan. Despite the dangers, volcanic activity can be useful. Water heated by molten rock that is deep underground supplies much of the country with hot springs, called *onsen*. Tourist resorts, which have been developed around *onsens*, are popular for bathing, and the natural hot water is sometimes used for cooking and even central heating.

For about three months, from mid-September, coastal Japan is at risk from typhoons. A strong typhoon can cause disastrous floods and landslides by bringing driving rain and hurricane-force winds.

Mountains, many densely forested, occupy 66 per cent of the land surface of Japan. They run mainly down through the western side of the islands like a backbone, so the majority of the population live on the flatter land towards the east.

Heavily dependent upon imports of raw materials, especially oil, Japan grows enough food to feed itself. However, with the rising cost of home-grown food, Japan is relying increasingly on produce from overseas.

> 'In 1959 a typhoon blew our roof off. We had to shelter in the local school with the rest of our neighbourhood.' – Yoshiko Ishihara, resident of Okazaki city.

The water in Chinoike hot spring, in Kyushu, is coloured by the minerals inside it. 'Chinoike' means 'pond of blood'.

Hot summer plains

Lying on the flat Okazaki plain, where the rivers Yahagi and Oto meet, Okazaki has everything to make it an ideal place to live.

Typical of other towns in the region, Okazaki has both agriculture and industry existing side by side. Rice, soybeans, mushrooms, grapes and strawberries are cultivated not far from factories producing cars, machinery, chemicals, knitted goods and textiles. A good supply of white granite from the nearby Mikawa hills has long made Okazaki famous for its stone-carvers, whose age-old industry is still successful.

Spring in Okazaki finds city parks filled with people picnicking beneath blossoming cherry trees. In the autumn, strollers flock to admire the blazing red Japanese maple trees. The muggy summer sends holidaymakers to the nearby beaches and, in winter, many young people go up to the ski resorts in the mountains in neighbouring regions such as Gifu and Nagano.

This stone-carver, in Okazaki, is making a lantern for decorating a Japanese garden.

Women in Okazaki Park ▶ have a picnic under the cherry blossom.

'My class goes out to paint pictures of the cherry blossoms in Okazaki park. So do schoolchildren from nearly every school in town.' – Sachiko Ishihara, 10 years old.

▼ *Rice fields outside Okazaki after the harvest.*

Okazaki citizens are proud of their city and their natural surroundings, and they have chosen certain local birds, flowers and trees as city mascots. Okazaki's bird is the black-and-white Japanese wagtail. Its flower is the lovely purple wisteria blossom. Okazaki's tree is the tall Mikawa black pine, some of which are found along surviving sections of the old Tokaido road.

13

A cooler valley

The cooler mountain climate of the Kiso valley means the cherry blossoms come out later in Narai than in Okazaki. It usually snows only on the mountains, but winters can be bitter, with temperatures as low as –20 ℃. As many a local farmer will tell you, 'It's too cold for snow'. The farmers of Narai grow rice, vegetables and fruit, but there are few other natural resources in the Kiso valley. Although the area is densely wooded, the local forestry industry is in decline. The area's most profitable resource is now its natural beauty. Many hikers and campers visit Narai during the summer and skiers go to its ski resorts in winter.

Autumn in the Kiso valley, where the surrounding mountains are among the highest in Japan.

The Kiso valley's streams and rivers, notably the Kiso river itself, are famous among Japan's many anglers. Several species of freshwater fish are common in the area. Trout, for example, is currently being raised on local fish farms to ensure a plentiful supply. A tributary of the Kiso river, the Narai river, flows through Narai, and is popular with local anglers.

The Kiso river can flow very fast, especially after rain. Too dangerous for boat transport, some sections are popular for canoeing, including over the white-water rapids.

▲ *The Narai river, at the bottom of the photo, flows past farmhouses near the village. The farmers' vegetable plots are beside the river.*

'Some years up here it freezes, others I've had my crops flooded. But when I think of summer-time, I wouldn't live anywhere else.' – Masao Furukuwa, farmer.

▲ *Narai's landscape is ideal for camping.*

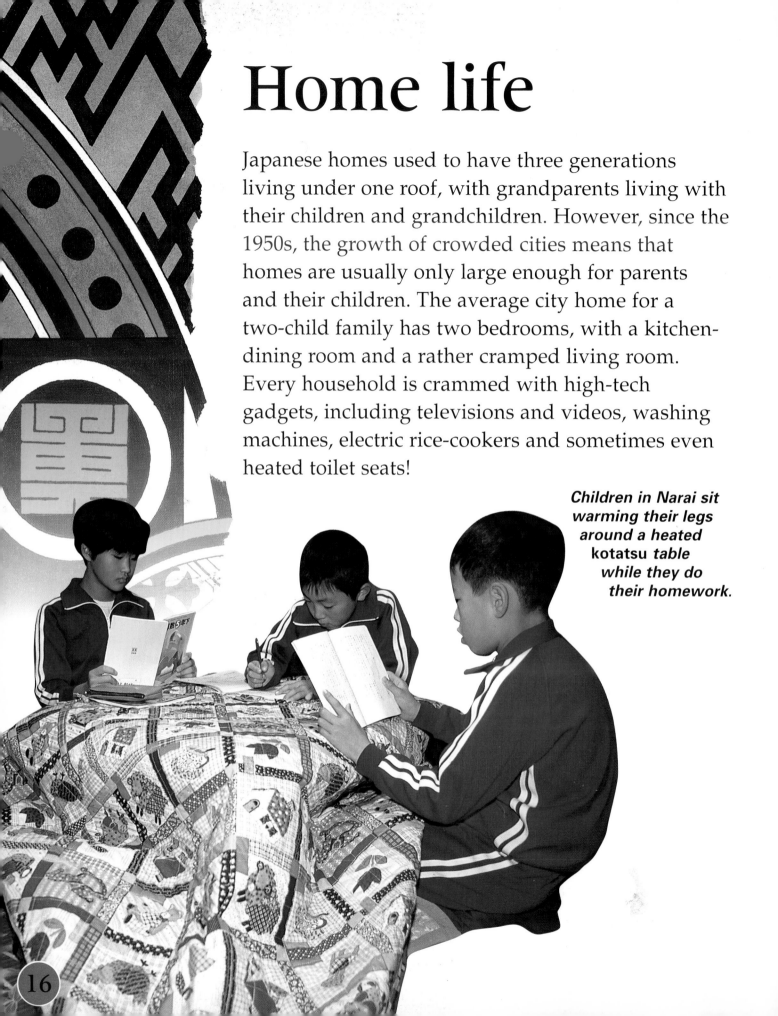

Home life

Japanese homes used to have three generations living under one roof, with grandparents living with their children and grandchildren. However, since the 1950s, the growth of crowded cities means that homes are usually only large enough for parents and their children. The average city home for a two-child family has two bedrooms, with a kitchen-dining room and a rather cramped living room. Every household is crammed with high-tech gadgets, including televisions and videos, washing machines, electric rice-cookers and sometimes even heated toilet seats!

Children in Narai sit warming their legs around a heated kotatsu table while they do their homework.

Yet only newer homes have central heating. Older houses use oil-stoves or electric heaters. In winter, many people sit snugly around a low table called a *kotatsu*, which has quilts around the side and a heater underneath.

▲ *A futon bed on* **tatami** *mat flooring.*

The Japanese live at floor level. A traditional floor is covered with smooth, springy matting called *tatami*. People sit at low tables on cushions placed on the tatami floor. Floors are always clean, because no one ever wears shoes at home.

Members of each family take a nightly bath in a square tub filled with piping hot water. However, the bath is just for soaking, not washing in, because the bath-water is shared. So no one enters the tub without having washed first. Until recently, many households had no baths, and people went to the *sento* (the public bath house) instead. The *sento* is still popular today – there's nothing like gossiping with neighbours in a large hot bath!

▼ *This is an* **ofuro,** *a traditional Japanese bath. This one is made of fragrant cedar wood.*

Traditional Japanese beds consist of mattresses on the floor, called futons. These are rolled up in the morning and put away in a cupboard for the day. Futons are still used, but sofas and Western-style beds are now also common.

Home life in Okazaki

Okazaki has both modern blocks of flats and older houses. Small families usually live in the flats, but in the older houses, grandparents, parents and children often all live together. Near the car assembly plant where he works, Kunio Ishihara shares an old house with his wife, mother and three children.

Every evening, the family eat together around a Western-style kitchen table using chopsticks. Supper always includes rice, pickles and miso soup, which accompany main dishes of fish or meat. The children also like Western-style food, especially hamburgers, but their grandmother can't even bring herself to taste it. On special occasions, everyone loves to eat *sashimi*, which are delicate mouthfuls of raw fish dipped in soy sauce.

Ten-year-old Sachiko helps her mother clear up, while her father and thirteen-year-old brother Koichi watch television. Eight-year-old Kentaro is upstairs playing computer games, but his mother will soon be up to see that he's done his homework.

'When I was a girl, my father was the boss. But my mother ruled the house and family budget. He used to hand her his monthly pay and she gave him his pocket money.'
– Hiroko Saito, 36 years old.

Sachiko and Kentaro eat sushi – small pieces of raw fish rolled with rice inside a leaf of dried seaweed.

Hiroshi Saito's family lives on the ninth floor of a block of flats. Twelve-year-old Harumi and her brother Junichi, nine, wish they saw more of their father, but by the time Hiroshi comes home from work, they are asleep.

Mrs Saito has a part-time office job, so for supper, she saves time by microwaving a supermarket supper. In Japan, men still rule the roost. When Hiroshi comes home, he might expect his wife to put out his *nemaki* (night clothes) and prepare his bath. Having demanded his supper, he might let her clear up afterwards. As in many younger families, however, Hiroshi devotes some of his little free time to sharing household chores.

Sachiko and Kentaro enjoy a quiz programme on television. Every Japanese household has at least one television – the bigger the better!

AVERAGE MONEY EACH HOUSEHOLD SPENDS A MONTH

Okazaki:	342,004 yen

Source: *Japan Economic Year Book,* 1995

Home life in Narai

The main street of Narai is lined with old wooden houses. It is so quiet that it looks as though only elderly people and babies live here. During the daytime, most of the villagers work outside the village. Some travel as far as Matsumoto, the area's largest town. Young children are looked after by their grandparents. Many families still live in old wooden farmhouses outside the village. A few still have a hole up in the high ceiling to let out the smoke from the *irori*, a square, sunken, stone fireplace in the living-room.

There are few shops along the main village street. Most people in Narai own a car and drive to large, local supermarkets to do their main shopping and stock their freezers.

Akio Watanabe is a lacquerware craftsman who lives on the main village street. Akio lives in a house he shares with his parents, his wife, his ten-year-old son Yoshi, and his twelve-year-old daughter Naoko. Supper in Narai is not quite the same as in Okazaki. Local river fish is available, which, in the Watanabe household, is caught by Yoshi and his father over the weekend. In season, there are

'It's not always easy living in an old wooden house like ours. We have a lot of repairs and our heating bills are high.'
– Akio Watanabe, lacquerware craftsman.

▼ *Children warm themselves before an* irori *fireplace. The kettle is set to boil for tea.*

sometimes stews of wild boar. There are also often dishes of mountain potatoes and vegetables grown by a local farmer.

The farmer, Mr Furukawa, lives with his wife in the farmhouse his grandfather was born in. They have a state pension which they add to by growing vegetables. Now grown up, the Furukawa's children left for Tokyo thirty years ago, during the late sixties. Life is more comfortable for the Furukawas than when they were young, but lonelier. They look forward to family visits in summer and at New Year, when they hear all about a city world they have only seen on television.

Old shop fronts along Naraijuku, the main street in Narai village. These shops have been recently restored to look as they did a century ago.

AVERAGE MONEY EACH HOUSEHOLD SPENDS A MONTH	
Narai:	327,456 yen

Source: *Japan Economic Year Book*, 1995

Japan at work

Take a look around you. How many things can you see that say 'Made in Japan'? It's likely that you'll find a computer, stereo, compact disc-player, video, television or tape deck that is Japanese. Someone in your house may own a Japanese watch or camera, or play a musical instrument made in Japan, or have a car that is Japanese. If you play computer games, the hardware and software might be Japanese too. All these high-tech industries employ many Japanese workers. Other giant industries in Japan include steel, heavy machinery, chemical and shipbuilding. Nearly all the electronics goods made around the world today contain some Japanese parts.

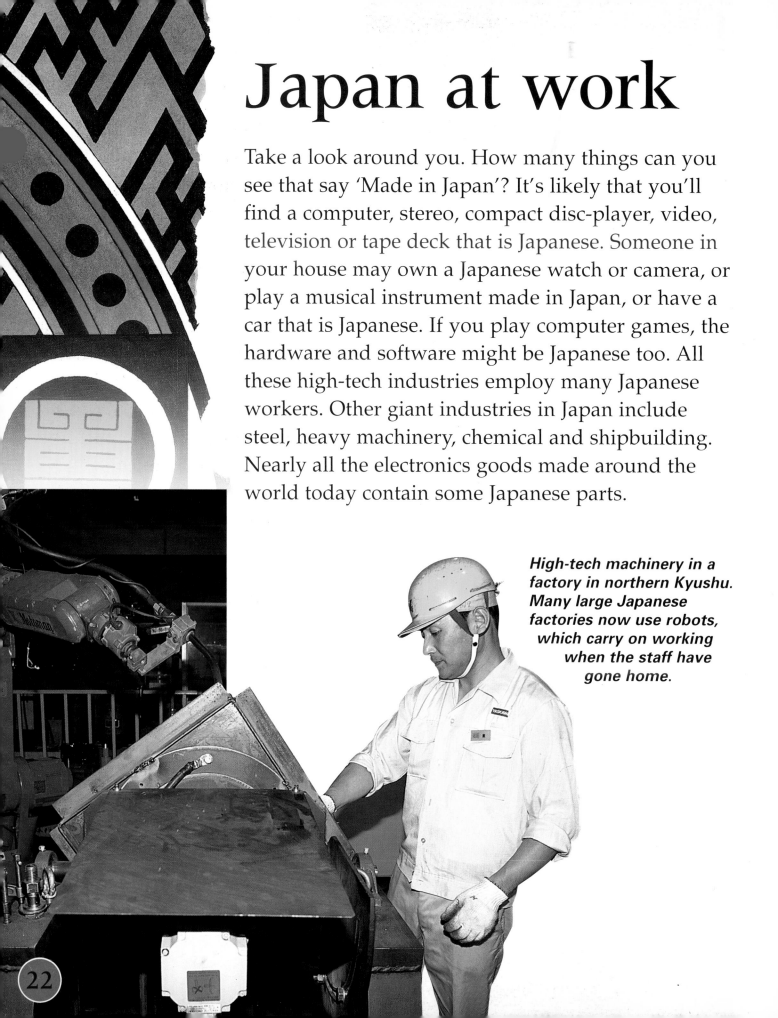

High-tech machinery in a factory in northern Kyushu. Many large Japanese factories now use robots, which carry on working when the staff have gone home.

▲ *Office workers on their way to work in Tokyo.*

WORK IN JAPAN	
Type of work	(percentage of population)
Agriculture:	6
Manufacturing:	33.9
Services:	60.1
Average working hours per week:	36.8
Average working hours per year:	1,913 (one week's paid holiday)

Source: *Facts and Figures Japan* (Foreign Press Centre, 1995)

The success of Japanese goods worldwide is due to sheer hard work. Until recently, working long hours, six days a week was regarded as normal by Japanese workers. One of the consequences of too much work, however, is too much production. During the 1980s, the Japanese government started to reduce working hours, so most big companies now work five days a week. However, smaller companies still often work long daily hours, with only one day off.

Since many small manufacturing companies depend on larger ones for their livelihood, they compete fiercely with each other for business. Such small factories are often called 'sweat-shops'. Workers flocking to Japan from poorer countries are often employed either in these or the construction industry.

Meanwhile, the position of women in Japan's work-force is very different from other industrialized countries. About a third of working women only work part time, and only very few become managers.

◀ *This man is using a tractor to plant rice seedlings, a job that used to be done by hand.*

Work in Okazaki

Okazaki is a centre for textile, car, machinery and chemical production, but it is also famous for work in traditional crafts that are centuries old. These products include painted festival banners, fireworks, and the carved wooden Buddhist altars that are found in most Japanese homes. Stone carving, especially garden ornaments, is another traditional industry in which Okazaki leads Japan. Another famous traditional product is miso, a nourishing soybean paste used in soups and seasonings. Since Okazaki is also a farming area, it is not unusual to see rice paddies alongside blocks of flats.

Most people in Okazaki, whatever type of work they do, work long hours. Office workers, like Hiroshi Saito, usually work until at least 9 pm. Saito has an hour's journey to work every day, so that by the time he gets home, at about 10 pm, his children are asleep. But working hours are getting shorter, and now Saito only has to work every other Saturday.

A modern miso factory. Miso paste has been made in Okazaki for centuries. It is made from fermented, ground soybeans.

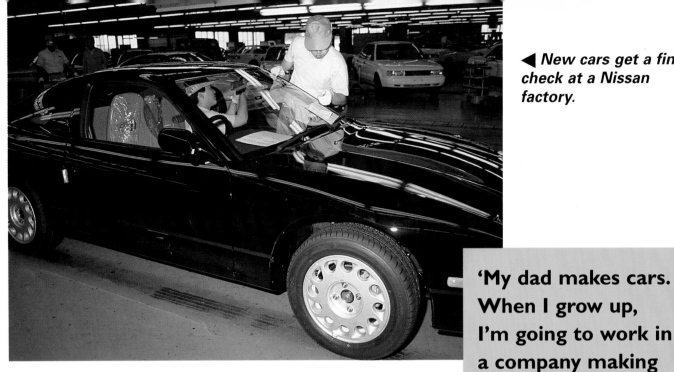

New cars get a final check at a Nissan factory.

'My dad makes cars. When I grow up, I'm going to work in a company making computer games.'
– Kentaro Ishihara, 8 years old.

Mr Ishihara is a foreman in a car assembly plant. Ishihara believes he is lucky to have a forty-hour working week because it means that he gets home in time to have supper with his family. Like most Japanese firms, Ishihara's company is organized with an order of rank, with senior and junior workers.

People who work in companies in Okazaki, as elsewhere in Japan, are promoted according to their age rather than their ability. They can expect employment for their entire working life. Larger companies provide many benefits, often including housing. In return, they expect a worker's complete loyalty. This sometimes means working overtime with no extra pay. These days, however, redundancies are becoming more frequent in Japan. In a solid company like his, Mr Ishihara is secure. But in many companies, the old 'lifetime employment system' is on the way out.

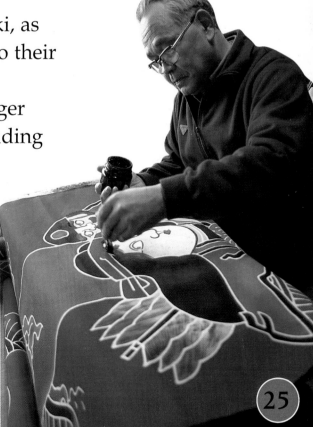

This banner is being painted for a festival such as Boys Day.

25

Work in Narai

In the past, the forests around Narai, which belong to the government, employed thousands of workers. But as the demand for timber grew, Japan began importing cheaper wood from abroad, so the livelihoods of many people in forested areas like Narai dwindled.

This timber yard in the Kiso valley has lost much work due to imports of cheaper wood.

The Kiso forests are famous for *hinoki* (Japanese cedar) trees. These trees are sacred to the Japanese, so they are felled to build Shinto shrines, and to make a variety of local wooden products. Another craft using local types of wood is Japanese lacquer.

Mr Watanabe is one of several lacquer craftsmen in Narai. Lacquer is a varnish with a very high gloss, which is usually red or black. The lacquering process is painstakingly slow and careful, since the gleaming surface must be perfect. Mr Watanabe learnt his craft from his father, and now produces trays, boxes and bowls. He belongs to a lacquerware co-operative which groups craftsmen together. The goods are distributed to shops around Japan, and the craftsmen share the profits.

In agriculture, the Narai area shares the same problems as Japan in general. Out of the 4 million people still working on farms, 63 per cent are over 55 years old. Mr Furukawa and his wife, who are 65 and 68 years old, are typical of local farmers. Their children chose more secure jobs in the city rather than continuing the family tradition of farming. Although some of their neighbours still cultivate rice, the Furukawas gave it up to concentrate on the growth of *sansai*, or mountain vegetables. They also grow *kaki* (persimmon fruit) trees and sell the dried fruit to local shops and supermarkets. Every winter, the Furukawas hang strings of bright orange *kaki* to dry on the eves of their old wooden farmhouse.

'A lot of my friends want to work in the city when they grow up. Not me. I want to stay and be a craftsman like my dad.' – Yoshi Watanabe, 10 years old.

◀ ▲ *Freshly painted lacquer bowls in a Narai workshop. To ensure an even coat, craftsmen use a special brush, tipped with human hair.*

Going to school

All Japanese children must go to school between the ages of six and fifteen. Most begin at four years old at nursery school. Starting elementary school at six, they then enter junior high school at twelve years old. At fifteen, over 90 per cent go to senior high school for four years. After this, about one-third will go on to university and training colleges. The fierce competition to enter senior schools and universities, however, is a serious problem in Japan's education system. Children have to pass entrance examinations with extremely high scores. Even some nursery schools require three year olds to take and pass entrance tests!

When exams draw near, pupils' workloads increase dramatically. Most attend *juku* (cram school) for about two hours after normal school, and then have too much homework for a good night's sleep. The Japanese call this 'examination hell'. Complaints about children's workloads recently, however, have meant that the amount of pressure on children in the education system is beginning to drop.

This boy is practising the art of calligraphy to improve his handwriting.

> 'These days, school kids have to work, work, work. With all that education, they hardly go outdoors any more.'
> – Masao Furukawa, 72 years old.

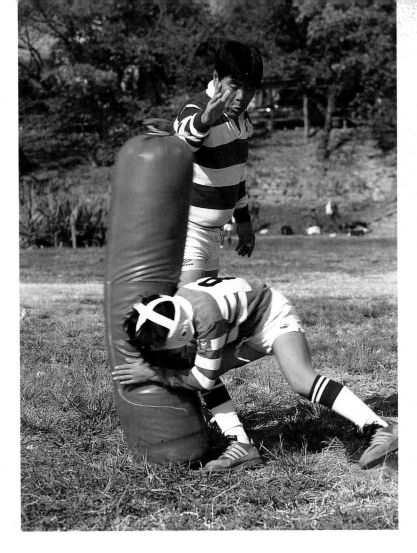

A young rugby player and his coach in Okazaki. Like football, rugby has suddenly grown very popular in Japan over the past ten years.

Schools still have time for music, arts and crafts, as well as games, swimming and athletics. Japan is famous for martial arts, and most schoolchildren, including girls, practise some form of martial art at school. Martial arts are taught to encourage self-discipline.

Japanese children learn to fend for themselves at a young age. Elementary pupils travel to school on their own, while children under six are escorted by elder children. The school system in Japan produces very high standards of education, and Japanese schoolchildren achieve the highest standards in the world in maths and science. They show great enthusiasm for learning, and truancy from school is very rare.

AFTER-CLASS ACTIVITIES	
	Pupils who take part in activities
Watching television	75.6%
Reading magazines and comics	64.2%
Outdoor sports	42.4%
Listening to music	34.4%
Reading books	27.5%
Hobbies	26.2%
Source: *Facts and Figures Japan* (Foreign Press Centre, 1995)	

School in Okazaki

Okazaki has plenty of schools, from nursery level right through to university. Kunio Ishihara's children go to schools near their home. Wearing white cotton sun-hats and bright-red school-bags on their backs, like most elementary school pupils, Sachiko and Kentaro catch the bus each morning at 8.30 am. Unlike their elder brother Koichi, they don't wear a uniform yet. Koichi wears the standard dark-blue uniform of pupils at high school, which is modelled on German naval-academy uniforms of the nineteenth century. The jacket of the girls' uniform has a sailor collar with white edges.

Koichi cycles to Kozan Junior High School, which has its own bicycle racks. Like his younger brother and sister, he goes on many school outings to local factories, museums and places of interest. Every summer, both elementary and junior high school pupils go on school holidays, including camping.

Girls discuss electronics at Kozan Junior High School, in Okazaki.

▲ *Kendo is a martial art based on samurai sword skills. It is practised by both boys and girls at Kozan Junior High School.*

Koichi is very keen on baseball, a sport played in schools all over the country. In Japan, boys play baseball and girls play volleyball. The best players are singled out to join teams that compete in national finals. Koichi also learns Kendo, a martial art based on samurai sword skills. His school runs a wide range of *kurabu* (clubs) to allow pupils to pursue hobbies and activities after school.

Okazaki's school pupils are responsible for tidying their own classrooms every day, and also for giving the whole school a thorough cleaning once a month. This teaches them to work together as a team, which is considered very important in Japan.

▼ *The main building of Kozan Junior High School, in Okazaki.*

'Western kids are luckier than us. We have to use Chinese characters. No wonder we have to work so hard at school!' – Koichi Ishihara, 13 years old.

31

School in Narai

There is only one school in Narai, which is an elementary school. So high-school pupils have to take the train to the nearby town of Yabuhara. Some senior high-school students may have to travel further along the line as far as Matsumoto, the area's largest town. They usually cycle to Narai station and leave their bicycles in a specially provided parking area, along with adults taking the train to work. Nowhere in Japan is too far from a school for a child to get to, which is why 90 per cent of the population were able to read and write as long ago as 1912. Children from a village without a high school, like Narai, simply travel to somewhere that has one.

▲ *Off to school early in the morning in Narai. All pupils cycling to school have to wear white crash helmets.*

▼ *Pupils from Narai on a school outing to the great hall of Todaiji temple, in Nara.*

▲ *These pupils are discussing a geometry project at Narai Elementary School.*

'What I like best at school is baseball. If I practise hard, one day I'll be in the national high school finals.' – Yoshi Watanabe, 10 years old.

There is little difference between the programmes of the schools in Narai and Yabuhara, and the schools in Okazaki. Children from Narai, however, such as Naoko Watanabe, may have more trouble in finding a cram school when they need one than children from Okazaki. Naoko Watanabe is soon starting junior high school, and is about to sit the entrance examination. To prepare for the exam, Naoko is given extra tuition a few hours a week at her home by a local teacher.

The choice of after-school club activities is more limited in Narai than in Okazaki, but a new football club has just started up, which Naoko's brother, Yoshi, is looking forward to joining. Football has recently become a craze in Japan. The village school also arranges outings for pupils. The Watanabe children are looking forward to a school bus trip this spring, when they will be taken to see the great temples of Nara and Kyoto.

Japan at play

FAVOURITE HOBBIES AND ACTIVITIES

	Percentage of adults who take part in activities
Watching videos	44.5
Music (radio, tapes, CDs)	41.7
Gardening	33.2
Going to the cinema	30.1
Video games	28.7
Pachinko	28.1
Going to concerts	22
Watching sports	20.7
Weaving, knitting, needlecraft	17.4
DIY, carpentry	15.4

Source: *White Paper on Leisure*, Japanese Leisure Development Centre, 1993

As working hours are gradually being reduced, the Japanese have more leisure time than ever before.

Almost every household has a radio and at least one television. The Japanese are also keen readers, often on the train to work. Large numbers of books are published every year, but they are far outnumbered by the number of magazines. Comics are more popular in Japan than anywhere else in the world, with millions of copies sold every week.

The Japanese are keen tourists, at home and abroad. Every weekend, millions take to the roads for outings, sightseeings and picnics.

Karaoke is a Japanese invention, which is often part of an outing, or even a wedding. Another popular pastime is *pachinko*, an upright pinball game played in special arcades.

◀ *Spectators at a baseball game.*

Every Japanese city has a baseball stadium. Baseball, called yakkyu, *has been Japan's national sport since the 1900s.*

The Japanese are also very fond of theme parks and fun fairs, such as Tokyo Disneyland, which attracts millions of visitors every year.

Trips to the cinema remain very popular, although televisions and videos have taken some of the audiences away.

Sports and athletics are very popular, both to watch and take part in. Sumo is a unique and traditional form of Japanese wrestling that dates back 1,000 years and features jumbo-sized opponents. Although expensive, tickets for Tokyo's national sumo tournaments sell out months in advance. Many sumo fans are happy to see tournaments on television. Baseball, which was introduced from the USA at the end of the nineteenth century, is Japan's national sport. Another popular sport, which has seen a sudden and fantastic rise in popularity during the 1990s is football.

Leisure time in Okazaki

Most people in Okazaki like to get out of the city at weekends and in holiday time. Many families, like the Ishihara family, enjoy driving out to the nearby Mikawa hills. They often have lunch there with relatives in a scenic restaurant. There is also a popular *onsen* hotel in the hills, where the Ishihara family spend a couple of days over New Year. This summer, the family are going to take a week's holiday on the island of Shikoku, where they will stay in a beach resort.

'My hobby is pottery. My pot in the Okazaki Children's Arts Museum won a prize.'
– Junichi Saito, 9 years old.

◀ *Junichi Saito practising his pottery at the Children's Art Museum.*

▲ *The Children's Art Museum in Okazaki, where children can do pottery, painting and many other crafts.*

CLOTHES WORN IN OKAZAKI

Leisure time:	**Casual clothes, tracksuits, jeans, trainers.** **Some emphasis on fashion.** *Yukata* **(cotton kimono) worn by both men and women at summer festivals.**
Formal occasions:	**Kimono or Western formal wear for both men and women.**

This Shinto festival is called Shichi-go-san, which means 'seven-five-three'. Children of these ages dress in their best clothes for blessings at shrines.

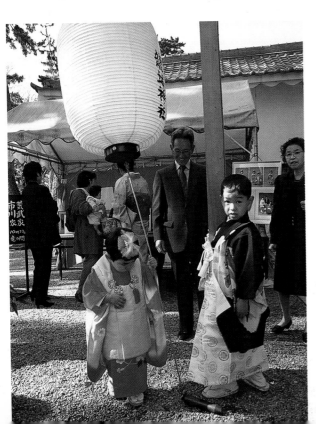

Although few people have gardens in Okazaki, many people like to shape *bonsai* trees, which are miniature trees. *Bonsai* trees are kept at about half a metre high, and they must be carefully cut and wired to stunt their growth.

Traditional arts are also popular in Okazaki. On Saturdays, after she has dropped the children off at the sports centre, Mrs Ishihara takes lessons on the samisen, a long-necked, three-stringed guitar.

Young people in Okazaki like both foreign and Japanese rock and pop music, and discos are popular in the city, although many drive to Nagoya for a bigger choice of discos. Their parents mostly prefer *enka* – a type of folk music that is well-suited for karaoke singing.

There are nineteen annual festivals in Okazaki, mostly connected to shrines, the Shinto places of worship. By far the most exciting is the Summer Festival in August, for which the townspeople turn up in force. In addition to colourful parades and costumed dancing, the events reach a climax with a firework display over the Sugo river. Using fireworks from Okazaki's famous Mikawa workshops, the display is the most spectacular in Japan.

Leisure time in Narai

In both Narai and Okazaki, as in villages and cities all over Japan, the Japanese are devoted television fans. In Narai, the Watanabe's television always seems to be on, even though no one seems to be watching it much of the time. Yoshi Watanabe never misses a moment of the hour's cartoon programmes when he comes home from school.

Life in Narai is so quiet that you can hear the Narai river from the main street. People looking for social entertainment have to go to Yabuhara, or even Matsumoto, to find restaurants or bars.

Children in Narai often take part in after-school activities, such as gymnastics classses, football or baseball. Computer games are also very popular.

Unlike city kids, the Watanabe children don't have to go very far for angling, hiking, camping, or skiing in the winter. But their biggest thrill is their summer trip to Tokyo Disneyland.

▼ *Hiking and camping are popular in the mountains and forests of the Kiso area.*

'What I like best on Sunday is when my dad takes me fishing. He gets quite annoyed if my fish are bigger than his!' – Yoshi Watanabe, 10 years old.

Kiso ponies, which ▶ used to be the only form of transport around Narai, are still raised in the area.

In the summer, the children of Narai, like many Japanese children, collect insects. They especially like collecting large, horned rhinoceros beetles and *semi*, the noisy Japanese cricket. The children put them in special clear plastic boxes, where they keep them as pets, feeding them bits of watermelon.

Elderly people in Narai are often visited by their children and grandchildren, who live in the cities, in the summer. The Furukawa grandchildren look to grandpa as a great authority on insects. He takes them to see fireflies, which are mostly gone from Japan's polluted cities. Another holiday highlight is when they visit a relative who raises Kiso ponies in the hills. These small, hardy ponies, a golden brown colour with black manes and tails, used to be the only means of transport in the region. Now they are trotted out during festival pageants in the Kiso area, and the Furukawa children ride them around the paddock.

CLOTHES WORN IN NARAI	
Leisure time:	Casual clothes, tracksuits, jeans, trainers. No emphasis on fashion. *Yukata* worn at summer festivals.
Formal occasions:	Kimono worn by nearly all women. Kimono or Western formal wear for men.

The future

After the Second World War, millions of Japanese left the countryside to work in the cities. Many cities, like Tokyo, grew too large, too fast. As a result, many Japanese now live in cramped homes, so their standard of living is fairly low.

To create more space, many cities are now constructing high-rise buildings, which are changing the appearance of Japanese cities. It may be sad that so many attractive old buildings are disappearing in Japan, but many have been destroyed by earthquakes. For example, Kobe's older districts were destroyed in the terrible earthquake of 1995, and in the Tokyo-Yokohama area, another devastating earthquake could happen at any moment. To reduce future damage, the Japanese now use earthquake-proof steel and concrete for new buildings.

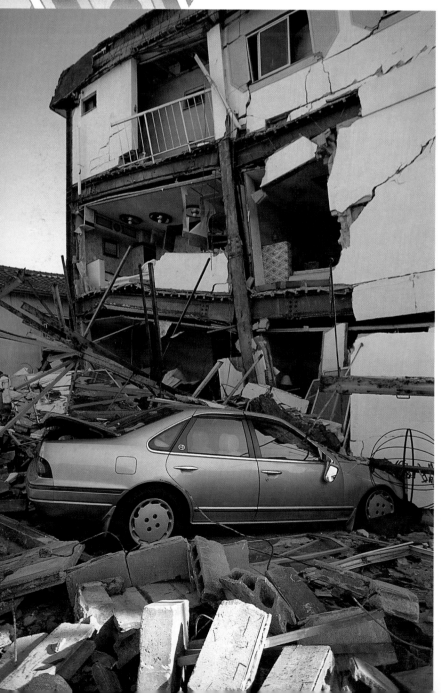

On 17 January 1995, whole districts of Kobe were destroyed by the most destructive earthquake in Japan since 1923. Over 5,000 people died.

Japan's future is bright, but its boom years are over. Its manufactured goods are more expensive, so exports have fallen. Japan also now has to compete with other rapidly industrializing countries around the Pacific area. But the country looks set to remain the world's leader in science and technology, and it is working on advances in computers and in bio-engineering.

Skyscrapers in Tokyo are designed to resist earthquakes.

There are plans to reduce the Japanese working week to forty hours, which will boost Japan's leisure industry. However, falling exports mean that unemployment is rising. In addition, robots are taking over assembly tasks in many Japanese factories. If too many factories use robots, many workers could be replaced by machines.

Becoming a world leader in only fifty years has, however, caused environmental damage. But major disasters in the past have made Japan take better care of pollution. The control of gas and fuel emissions is now very strict, and much has been done to ensure a cleaner future.

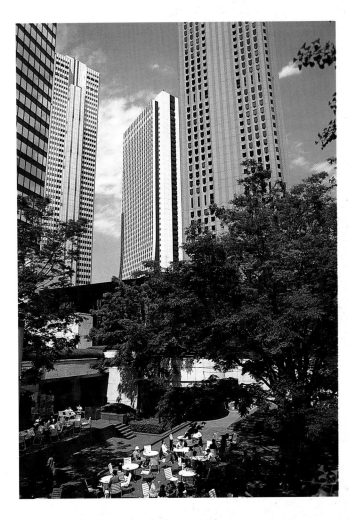

MAJOR EARTHQUAKES			
DATE	PLACE	DEATHS	STRENGTH (Richter scale)
23 September 1923	Tokyo	100,000+	no record
21 December 1946	Honshu	2,000	8.4
28 June 1948	Fukui	5,131	7.3
26 May 1983	N. Honshu	81	7.7
12 July 1993	Hokkaido	200+	7.7
17 January 1995	Kobe	5,400+	7.2

Source: *Facts and Figures Japan* (Foreign Press Centre, 1995)

The future of Okazaki

Okazaki is a thriving city which looks set to continue to grow in both wealth and population. Recently, a sharp increase in immigrant factory workers, particularly from South America and the Philippines, is making the city more international. Plans for the city include another city centre around the train station, and a new Okazaki Central Park, which will include facilities for culture, leisure and sports. Other major works include a new city hospital, a community welfare centre and a vast welfare building serving the whole of the region. Okazaki has also been chosen by the government as the base for a new multi-media network. This will be housed in a giant centre for local information and communications.

Two children from Umezono elementary school in Okazaki.

Okazaki's environment, like many other Japanese cities, has suffered from the city's growth. In Gamagori, once Okazaki's local beach resort, industrial waste made the water unsafe for swimming, and during the early 1970s, the beach had to be buried under a concrete seafront. However, Okazaki's citizens now put different kinds of rubbish out on different days, so that metal, glass, burnable and non-burnable rubbish is separated. Cans and glass are collected for recycling, which is considered vital throughout Japan. To recycle some of the glass, Okazaki's city council even runs a glass-blowing workshop, which is open to everyone.

▲ *The Okazaki fire department practises its fire drill.*

◄ *The concrete promenade of Gamagori, Okazaki's local beach resort, which was created after pollution ruined the original beach.*

The future of Narai

Thanks to efforts made to preserve its scenic beauty, Narai's future as a tourist attraction is quite safe and its popularity has increased during the past few years. A very old *sake* (Japanese rice wine) brewery along the main street has become a national landmark and the village's few businesses now include souvenir shops.

Apart from tourism, Narai's future is less certain. Japanese farmers have suffered from the growing amount of cheaper imports from abroad, especially since 1990, when the country's booming economy slowed down. Small shops like Narai's grocery, for example, are being increasingly threatened by large supermarkets. Some of these are importing goods directly from abroad, and selling them at rock-bottom prices.

▼ ▶ *A craftsman makes traditional wooden combs in the Kiso village museum.*

An increasing number of children will probably return to villages like Narai in the future, as communications and technology become more advanced.

Lacquerware production still thrives in Narai, but many other old crafts are dying out. The government is trying to preserve these traditional crafts, mainly by having older craftsmen working in museums. In the Kiso area, such crafts include the hand-tooling of wooden combs.

Local authorities near Narai have recently tried to attract people back from the cities by offering them attractive housing deals. So while many country people have left for the cities, city people are gradually moving to the country. The development of computer communications will soon make living and working in remote areas much easier than before. In the future, many more people will want to live in villages like Narai.

Glossary

Active volcano A volcano that is hot and likely to erupt.

Angler Someone who fishes with a rod and line.

Calligraphy The practice of handwriting as an art. The Japanese often hang large-lettered works of calligraphy, often poems, on the wall.

Fault A crack.

Hardware Equipment and machinery. Computer hardware refers to the computer itself and the printer, as well as any other equipment that makes up the system.

Industrialized A country where the economy is mainly based on industry.

Kimono A loose robe with wide sleeves and a broad sash.

Kurabu From the English word 'club'. Many modern Japanese words like this are of foreign (usually English) origin.

Manufacturing The production of goods.

Matsuri A Japanese religious festival.

Onsen A Japanese word meaning 'hot spring'. In volcanic areas in Japan, water sometimes comes naturally heated out of the ground.

Produce Pronounced <u>prod</u>-uce, this means crops, fruit, vegetables and foodstuffs produced from agriculture.

Resource Whatever the land has which people need in order to live and to make money. Water, wood, coal and minerals are all resources.

Richter scale A scale used for measuring earthquakes. Level three on the scale is strong enough to be felt, whereas level seven can topple buildings. The highest earthquake ever recorded measured 8.9 on the Richter scale.

Samurai Japanese warriors from medieval times. The samurai ruled Japan until 1868.

Services Work such as tourism and banking, that does not make goods but supplies people with services they need.

Software The programmes a computer needs to make it work. Computer games are software.

Textiles Materials used for making clothing. Cotton, wool, silk and artificial fibres such as lycra are all textiles.

Tributary A river or stream that feeds a bigger river.

Typhoon A storm with high winds and a great deal of rain. Typhoons occur in the China Sea and the Eastern Pacific down to the Philippines. They can often be disastrous.

Volcanic To do with volcanoes.

White-water rapids Rocks on the river bed form small waterfalls called rapids. Since the water can flow very fast in rapids, it becomes white with foam.

Yukata A cotton kimono worn in the summer.

Further information

Books to read

Area Resource Pack: Japan by Vincent Bunce (Stanley Thornes, 1995)

Country Fact Files: Japan by John Baines (Simon & Schuster Young Books, 1992)

Country Topics: Japan by Richard and Sheila Tames (Watts, 1994)

Modern Industrial World: Japan by Lesley Downer (Wayland, 1994)

Passport to Japan by Richard Tames (Watts, 1993)

Real World: Japan by Vincent Bunce (Watts, 1994)

Useful addresses

Japan Information and Cultural Centre, Japanese Embassy, 101–104 Piccadilly, London W1V OAH
Tel: 0171 465 6500

Japan National Tourist Organization, 167 Regent Street, London W1R 7FD
Tel: 0171 734 9638

VIDEOS

Japan 2000 (BBC, 1995/6)

PICTURE ACKNOWLEDGEMENTS

All photographs except the cover are by Jim Holmes, of Axiom Photographic Agency.

Cover photograph: Eye Ubiquitous (Frank Leather)

All map artwork is by Peter Bull.

Index

Page numbers in **bold** refer to photographs.